GW01403202

Original title:
Quiet Flickers Inside the Fae Cull

Author: Olivia Orav

ISBN HARDBACK: 978-1-80562-999-3
ISBN PAPERBACK: 978-1-80564-520-7

Veils of Enchantment in the Gloom

In shadows deep, where whispers sigh,
The veils of magic softly lie.
Around the trees, the secrets dance,
Inviting hearts to take a chance.

The moonlight spills on hidden streams,
Where soft enchantments weave through dreams.
Each glowing orb, a tale to tell,
Of ancient spells, in silence dwell.

The nightingale sings of unseen sights,
While starlit paths guide wayward flights.
With every step on ground so fair,
A promise hangs within the air.

Beneath the boughs, in twilight's grace,
The time-worn charms, a warm embrace.
In every shadow, lore remains,
A tapestry of joy and pains.

So linger here, where spirits twine,
In veils of night, let magic shine.
For in the gloom, with every turn,
A flicker glows, a heart will learn.

Flickers of the Forgotten Pathway

Along the path where memories wane,
Faint echoes stir, both sweet and plain.
With steps unheard, the past arrives,
In whispered dreams, the spirit thrives.

The lanterns glow with gentle gleam,
Awakening hopes, igniting a dream.
With every page turned by the night,
Flickers of joy, a guiding light.

Through tangled woods, the shadows creep,
In silence deep, where secrets sleep.
Yet every turn brings forth a spark,
To kindle warmth within the dark.

The journey calls with tender grace,
To seek the truth in every place.
For in the heart where wonders lay,
Flickers of love will light the way.

So wander forth on winding trails,
Embrace the magic that never fails.
For every step in twilight's glow,
Reveals the dreams we dare to sow.

Luminescent Echoes of the Timeless

In shadows thick where whispers weave,
The stars above begin to thieve.
Each glimmer calls, a ghostly tune,
As night unfolds beneath the moon.

A dance of light, eternal grace,
In every heart, a hidden place.
Where echoes linger, soft and bright,
And time, it bends in velvet night.

Through misty dreams and twilight's seam,
The world unwinds, a fleeting dream.
With every pulse, the moments gleam,
And weave together like a stream.

The ancient trees, they softly sigh,
As time drifts slowly, passing by.
With every glance, the past ignites,
In luminescent, frail delights.

So let us wander, hand in hand,
Through realms of magic, bright and grand.
In echoes lost, where silence plays,
We'll chase the night, the timeless ways.

Murmurs in the Undergrowth

In tangled roots where secrets lie,
The gentle rustle breathes a sigh.
Beneath the ferns, the whispers swell,
In every nook, a magic spell.

The nightingale soft notes entice,
As crickets chirp their syncopice.
The moonlight weaves through branches high,
Unfolding tales as shadows fly.

With every step, the forest hums,
A pulsing life that softly drums.
In every leaf, a story sways,
In murmurs where enchantment plays.

The roots entwine like hands in prayer,
Holding dreams in tender care.
Each breath a flutter, softly heard,
A testament in nature's word.

So linger here, where magic brews,
In undergrowth, where dreams infuse.
Let silence speak, let shadows gleam,
In whispered thoughts, we too will dream.

Dusk's Breath of Hidden Flickers

As twilight drapes the tired day,
In softest hues, the shadows play.
The fireflies dance, a fleeting kiss,
In dusk's embrace, a whispered bliss.

The sky ignites in amber glow,
While stars awaken, row by row.
In every glint, a story spins,
A tapestry where magic begins.

The breeze it carries, secrets old,
In twilight's arms, the night unfolds.
Each breath a sigh, both sweet and light,
As dreams arise, ready for flight.

Beneath the trees, the hush descends,
A tranquil calm as daylight ends.
In hidden flickers, life ignites,
As dusk unveils its hidden sights.

Let shadows linger, let them drift,
In every heartbeat, we find a gift.
For in this hour, the magic stirs,
And in our souls, the wonder purrs.

Magic Pulses Beneath the Earth

In depths unseen, where dreams abide,
The heartbeat of the world does hide.
Through roots and stone, a current flows,
A mystic hum that softly glows.

The ancient soil, with tales to tell,
In hidden paths where shadows dwell.
Each pulse, a whisper, deep and wise,
A secret shared 'neath starry skies.

As mountains rise and rivers wend,
The magic pulses without end.
In every crack, in every seam,
Life breathes anew, a quiet dream.

The earth responds, in murmurs sweet,
With every tremor, life's heartbeat.
A world alive, beneath our feet,
In hidden wonders, hearts will meet.

So let us dig into the night,
To find the glow of deep delight.
For magic pulses, fierce and true,
In every heartbeat, me and you.

Choreographed Candles of Enchantment

In the garden where shadows play,
Candles twirl in soft ballet.
Their flicker tells a tale of light,
A dance of wonders through the night.

Whispers rise, a shimmering flow,
As petals gleam with silver glow.
Each flame a wish, each spark a song,
In this embrace, where dreams belong.

With every step, the magic sighs,
Reflecting secrets in the skies.
An orchestra of flares and hues,
A symphony of warm renews.

Encircled by the moon's soft gaze,
The world transforms in golden haze.
Through twinkling light, our hearts entwined,
In this enchanted space, aligned.

So let us waltz beneath the stars,
Amongst the smoke of ancient jars.
With candles choreographed so fine,
We lose ourselves in love's design.

Muffled Radiance in the Starlit Ferns

Beneath the cloak of leafy green,
The magic whispers, soft and keen.
In ferns where flickering fairies dwell,
The night conceals its radiant spell.

Each star a wink, each shadow sings,
Of hidden truths and gentle things.
Amidst the hush, the wonders wake,
The helm of night, a calm embrace.

Moonbeams drip like silver dew,
Igniting dreams, both old and new.
In this realm of whispering light,
The world feels perfectly right.

The air is thick with magic's breath,
As time stands still, defying death.
A solace found in nature's weave,
In star-kissed ferns, we dare believe.

So tread with care, with heart and mind,
For treasures lie, yet undefined.
Muffled radiance, an angel's kiss,
In starlit ferns, we find our bliss.

Hushed Gleams of Woodland Dreams

In the heart of the whispering wood,
Lie ancient tales, where legends stood.
Hushed gleams flicker through the trees,
Drawn by a breeze, like gentle pleas.

Mossy carpets, soft and plush,
In dreams where time can barely rush.
Every glance a new surprise,
In nature's arms, wisdom lies.

The brook babbles secrets low,
A lullaby that ebbs and flows.
With starlit paths that softly gleam,
They lead us through this woodland dream.

Silent sighs and echoes hum,
As fireflies weave a dance that's spun.
In twilight's grace, the soul can soar,
Lost in the magic, forevermore.

So tread lightly, find the way,
Through hushed gleams at the close of day.
For in each step, a truth it seems,
Awaits us in these woodland dreams.

Twilight's Embrace on Gossamer Wings

As twilight drapes its velvet veil,
The air is thick with secret tales.
Upon gossamer wings, we fly,
Through dusky realms where shadows lie.

The sun sinks low, a golden orb,
In twilight's grasp, our hearts absorb.
Each fluttered leaf and whispered breeze,
Carries the hints of mysteries.

Softly echoes of laughter ring,
As twilight dances on fragile wings.
With every heartbeat, dreams unfurl,
In the twilight mist, we twirl and swirl.

Lost in the glow of fading light,
We seek the magic of the night.
For in this hour so sweet and rare,
We find the worlds beyond compare.

So let us linger, let us soar,
On gossamer wings, forever more.
In twilight's embrace, we reside,
As dreams and light become our guide.

Ethereal Whispers of the Woods

In twilight's embrace, the shadows sigh,
Leaves murmur secrets as soft winds fly.
Moonbeams dance lightly, just out of reach,
Nature's own lullaby, words without speech.

The brook babbles gently, a melody clear,
Echoing stories only the trees hear.
Creatures of night come alive in the gloom,
Crickets' sweet symphonies fill up the room.

Among ancient roots, where the wildflowers bloom,
Sweet scents of magic drift through the gloom.
Footsteps quite gentle tread paths of the wise,
Revealing the worlds hidden deep in their eyes.

Shimmering Essence of Unseen Spirits

In the hush of the night, where the mists weave,
Glimmers of magic, the heart must believe.
Dancing like fireflies, flickers of light,
Whispering tales of the ethereal night.

Soft shadows entwine in the cool evening air,
Living their stories with utmost care.
Translucent figures, they spin and they twirl,
Wrapping the forest in a silvery swirl.

Echoes of laughter cascade through the trees,
Brought on the wings of the softest of breezes.
The spirit of joy flutters wild and free,
In realms where the unseen entwines with the sea.

Tranquil Gleams Among the Trees

Sunlight filters through, a golden embrace,
Illuminating paths in this mystical space.
Whispers of breezes caress every leaf,
Warming the heart with a sweet, gentle belief.

Where sunlight and shadows create a soft play,
Nature awakens, inviting the day.
Each rustle and murmur, a sound to behold,
Stories unfold through the ages retold.

Graceful the dance of the branches above,
Cradling the heavens with purpose and love.
Moments are treasures, wrapped in a sigh,
As tranquility reigns in the woods nearby.

Veiled Lights in the Heart of the Forest

Beneath arching boughs, where the silence sings,
Veiled lights flicker softly, like fragile wings.
The heart of the forest, a glimmering guise,
Hides echoes of wonder, unseen to our eyes.

Intrigues of twilight compose in the dark,
Each rustling secret, a soft, joyful spark.
Pathways of shadows lead deeper within,
Where the magic of dusk with the dawn does begin.

In this realm of enchantment, peace reigns supreme,
Life breathes a chorus, a tender dream.
So linger a moment, and let your heart soar,
In the veiled lights whispering tales evermore.

Twinkling Eyes of the Never-Was

In the shadows where dreams softly tread,
Whispers of wishes and tales long dead.
Eyes like lanterns, casting a glow,
Twinkling with secrets only they know.

Memories dance in the moon's sweet embrace,
Lost in the echoes of time and space.
A flicker of laughter, a shimmer of tears,
Each gaze a portal to long-lost years.

Night wraps around like a silken shroud,
Murmurs of magic rise soft and loud.
From shadows emerge the voices of yore,
In twinkling eyes, a forgotten lore.

The stars hold their breath in the stillness above,
As we gather tales of sorrow and love.
In glimmers and flashes, they weave a net,
Twinkling eyes beckon, never forget.

So let your heart follow the spark of your soul,
Into the realms where whispers console.
In narratives stitched with threads of the past,
Twinkling eyes guide the dreams that will last.

Enchanted Breaths of Starlight

Upon the dawn, where the shadows retreat,
Enchanted breaths in the air bittersweet.
Starlight caresses the cheeks of the day,
Whispering secrets as it fades away.

Each beam a promise of magic unspun,
Adventures await, beneath one rising sun.
In the silence, soft murmurs collide,
Carrying wishes like waves of the tide.

With every heartbeat, a spark starts to grow,
Crimson and gold in the evening's warm glow.
The twilight ignites all the dreams we possess,
In enchanted breaths of starlight's caress.

As twilight's curtain descends from above,
The heartbeat of night sings a song of love.
In the tender sighs of the universe wide,
Lay the cosmic secrets in time's gentle glide.

So let your spirit, like starlight, refrain,
From clinging to doubt, from burying pain.
With every breath, let enchantment ignite,
Wrap you in wonders that shimmer at night.

Mysterious Gleams of the Dancing Leaf

In the forest where shadows and sunlight meet,
Mysterious gleams make the journey sweet.
Leaves flush with whispers, secrets untold,
In the dance of the breeze, their stories unfold.

With every rustle, an echo of grace,
Nature's soft laughter, a warm, safe place.
Colors collide in a vibrant ballet,
Each leaf a character in nature's play.

The branches sway gently, in tune with the skies,
Where dreams weave in patterns, where wonder lies.
In the glistening dew, the dawn's gentle sigh,
Awakening spirits that soar and fly.

In every turn, in each twist of the vine,
Synchronizing rhythms of stories divine.
Mysterious gleams beckon hearts to believe,
In the dance of the leaves, we learn to perceive.

So wander in pathways where wildflowers bloom,
Chasing the echoes that lift from their gloom.
In the vibrant embrace of the dancing leaf,
Find solace and wonder, let sorrow be brief.

Specters of Flickering Luminescence

In the depths where the shadows play games,
Specters arise with soft, whispering names.
Flickering lights in the depths of the night,
Guide us through darkness to realms full of light.

They waltz through the mist like a figment of dreams,
Bathing the world in their shimmering beams.
Time bends and sways, in a magical trance,
As specters of light lead us forth in a dance.

With each glowing flicker, a story unwinds,
Secrets of ages are where the heart finds.
A tapestry woven with threads of the years,
Flickering memories infused with our fears.

In the misty embrace, gentleness swirls,
Like whispers of magic where mystery unfurls.
As specters of flickering luminescence glow,
They beckon the dreamers, the seekers, the slow.

Step forth in the night, feel the rhythm's sweet pulse,
In specters of light, let your spirit convulse.
For in every twinkle, there lies a deep sense,
Of hope that shines bright in luminous suspense.

Vibration of the Lightbound Souls

In whispers soft as twilight's breath,
They dance upon the edge of death.
With every step, the echoes blend,
A harmony that knows no end.

Together bound, like stars in night,
Their spirits soar, a vibrant flight.
In luminous trails of silver hue,
They weave their tales, both old and new.

Through realms unseen, their laughter rings,
A testament to all life brings.
In sacred circles, energies flow,
As time stands still, and love will grow.

With every pulse, the cosmos sighs,
In strands of fate, the spirit lies.
Their union bright, a timeless song,
In every heart, they all belong.

So when the night seems dark and deep,
Remember souls that never sleep.
For in the silence, you may hear,
The lightbound calls that draw us near.

Humming Waves Beneath the Canopy

Beneath the leaves, a secret hum,
Where creatures stir and echo come.
In gentle sways, the branches creak,
A melody from nature's peak.

The sunlight filters, golden beams,
Awakening the world of dreams.
From every nook, a choir swells,
In harmony where magic dwells.

Each rustling leaf tells tales untold,
Of whispered paths in forests old.
In shimmering dance, the shadows play,
Recalling past in a subtle way.

The fragrance soft, of earth and rain,
Hums through the air like sweet refrain.
In twilight's glow, the night draws near,
And crickets chirp, the music clear.

So close your eyes and breathe it in,
Feel nature's pulse beneath your skin.
For here the waves of silence swell,
In hidden realms where wonders dwell.

Shadows Caressing the Ancient Wood

In twilight's grasp, the shadows glide,
They dance along the forest side.
With tender touch, they weave a tale,
Of ancient trees and winds that wail.

They whisper softly, secrets deep,
In every nook, where spirits sleep.
With roots entwined, the past holds sway,
In every breath, a life portrayed.

The light retreats as darkness reigns,
In every corner, memory remains.
As shadows stretch, the heart will yearn,
For wisdom lost, for lessons learned.

Yet in that gloom, there lies a spark,
A flicker bright, a love in dark.
For in the wood, both fierce and kind,
The shadows greet, entwined and blind.

So wander forth, through night and day,
Embrace the shadows, lose your way.
For in the ancient wood's embrace,
You'll find yourself in time and space.

Flickering Mirages of the Wild

In distant glades where spirits roam,
Mirages dance, a world of home.
With painted skies and wild allure,
A flicker bright, forever pure.

The sunlit beams, in colors bold,
Reveal the stories yet untold.
As fireflies spark the evening's air,
Each glow a wish, a dream laid bare.

Through rustling grass, the whispers flow,
Of echoes past, of seeds we sow.
In every heart, the wild resides,
With secrets deep where hope abides.

So chase the mirage, don't look back,
Embrace the path, stay on the track.
For in the flickers of the night,
You'll find your way, a guiding light.

In nature's arms, with joy you'll weave,
A tapestry of dreams to leave.
As twilight fades, let not hearts fear,
For wilds alive will ever endear.

Glistening Visions of the Sylvan Unseen

In shadows deep where secrets hide,
The forest breathes, a lullaby wide.
Each leaf a story, each branch a song,
In glistening visions, we find where we belong.

With silver dew on emerald blades,
Whispers of magic in twilight parades.
Creatures dance in the cool night air,
In sylvan realms, they gather, they share.

A flicker's light, a firefly's flight,
Guides the way through the soft, gentle night.
Lost in wonder, we drift and we roam,
In this enchanted wood, we find our home.

Moonlit paths where shadows entwine,
Each step we take feels utterly divine.
The rush of a stream, a wind's gentle sigh,
These glistening visions will never die.

In the heart of the woods, a promise now gleams,
A world that lives on in our wildest dreams.
With every dawn, a new tale will spin,
In the sylvan unseen, our journey begins.

Illuminated Whispers Beneath the Stars

Under the night, the cosmos sings,
A tapestry woven of celestial strings.
With silvered whispers, the stars take flight,
Guiding our hearts through the velvet night.

Each twinkling light like a story untold,
Of lovers and heroes, of brave and bold.
In the hush of the night, we lean in to hear,
The dreams of the ages, both distant and near.

A breeze carries secrets, a gentle embrace,
In illuminated spaces, we find our place.
The moon watches over with a smile so bright,
Cradling our hopes with her luminous light.

Glimmers of wisdom from ages long past,
In shadows and starlight, our souls are cast.
With every heartbeat, beneath this embrace,
We whisper our wishes to the stars' endless grace.

In this celestial dance, we find our way,
Illuminated whispers guide night into day.
Together we wander through dreams that we've spun,
Beneath the vast heavens, our souls become one.

Phosphorescence of the Forgotten Glade

Deep in the woods where few have tread,
A glade lies waiting, where dreams have fled.
In phosphorescent glow, the flowers bloom,
Casting soft light to dispel the gloom.

The ancient trees, with wisdom they share,
Stand sentry-like, in the cool night air.
With each whispered sigh, the earth seems to sigh,
A lullaby drifting, a tale to comply.

Moss blankets the ground, a verdant delight,
In the heart of the glade, all is made right.
Entranced by the shimmer, we watch and we wait,
For magic ignites, and our hearts resonate.

As fireflies dance in a jubilant trance,
We lose ourselves in this mystical chance.
Phosphorescent dreams, they weave and they swirl,
Like whispers of fate, our lives gently twirl.

Here in this haven, we find what is real,
In the phosphorescence, our spirits can heal.
A sanctuary hidden, where souls intertwine,
In the forgotten glade, forever we shine.

Resplendent Shimmers of the Dreamweavers

In twilight's embrace, where visions take flight,
The dreamweavers gather, igniting the night.
With threads of starlight, they spin and they weave,
Crafting rich dreams for those who believe.

A shimmer of magic in every soft sigh,
They lend us their wings, helping spirits to fly.
With whispers of hope, they dance through the air,
Creating a world that's wondrous and rare.

In the folds of the night, new stories ignite,
In the heart of the dreamers, we glimpse the delight.
Each spark of a wish, a new path to pursue,
Resplendent shimmers of all that is true.

Through the tapestry woven with laughter and tears,
We find healing light that dispels our fears.
With every breath taken, we join in their song,
In the realm of the dreamers, we all can belong.

Where shadows converge, and the light softly gleams,
Our hearts intertwine in the web of our dreams.
The night whispers gently, guiding us near,
As the resplendent shimmers of dreams reappear.

Echoes of the Glimmering Veil

In the hush of twilight's breath,
Whispers dance through silver trees,
Murmurs linger, time held fast,
Dreams entwined on gentle breeze.

Beyond the veil of moonlit glow,
Secrets weave in shadows deep,
Lost in tales of long ago,
Where ancient spirits softly weep.

Beneath the stars, a shimmer bright,
Echoes of a world once known,
Through the dark, a glimmering light,
Guiding souls that roam alone.

Where laughter fades, yet magic stays,
In every sigh of twilight's fall,
The haunting song, it gently plays,
A beckoning to heed the call.

In silent glades where shadows blend,
The secrets of the night are spun,
Echoes of a soft descend,
As dreams unfurl, the magic's begun.

Shining Threads in the Allusive Night

Upon a loom of starry skies,
The threads of night begin to weave,
Each shimmer holds a thousand sighs,
In whispers only night can leave.

Dancing fireflies trace their tales,
Illuminating paths unseen,
While the wind recites its gales,
On a stage where time has been.

Through tangled stars, a passage bright,
Threads of destiny intertwine,
In the fabric of endless night,
Hearts call softly, 'You are mine.'

Layered shadows, secrets spun,
Each pulse of magic filling air,
With every heartbeat, dreams begun,
In the silence, a lover's prayer.

As daylight fades, the colors blend,
In twilight's grasp, dreams take their flight,
Dare to follow, brave hearts extend,
For in the dark, shines allusive light.

Dimming Light of the Faery Heart

In the glen where whispers fall,
The faery heart begins to fade,
A soft glow, a fleeting call,
In twilight's hues, the magic laid.

Petals drift on gentle streams,
As laughter echoes through the night,
Once bright hopes held in silver dreams,
Now dimming in the gentle light.

Yet in the gloom, a spark still stirs,
A flicker born of ancient lore,
Through darkened paths where silence blurs,
A heartbeat waits beyond the door.

Through tangled roots and shadowed trees,
The faery heart, though faint, will guide,
In whispered vows upon the breeze,
A light remembered, love, our pride.

For deep within the fading light,
Lives an ember strong and true,
In darkest hours, we reclaim the sight,
With every breath, a promise due.

Ghostly Lights Casting Secrets

Across the moor where shadows lay,
Ghostly lights begin to twine,
With secrets held in soft decay,
As night unfolds its velvet line.

A shimmer blurs the edge of dreams,
Where ancient echoes stretch their hand,
Drawing forth the past, it seems,
In whispering winds, on ghostly land.

Through the veils of misty night,
These flickers tell of what once was,
The truth entangled with delight,
Unraveled softly, because.

Where phantoms waltz in tethered time,
Their stories dance on fragile air,
Each glimmer holds a hidden rhyme,
With layers of the past laid bare.

So heed the lights that softly glow,
In the stillness, listen near,
For ghostly whispers ebb and flow,
And secrets held will soon appear.

Elusive Shines of the Enchanted Path

In the forest deep, where shadows play,
Elusive shines guide the lost today.
A flicker here, a sparkle bright,
Whispers of magic, hidden from sight.

Beneath the boughs where secrets dwell,
Ancient tales they weave and tell.
Steps entwined in stories old,
Each glimmer whispers, be brave, be bold.

Through misty veils and bramble's hold,
Forgotten roads thus gently unfold.
With silver beams dancing light,
A pathway glimmers, what's wrong feels right.

Amidst the whispers, the night will bloom,
A lullaby calls from the beckoning gloom.
The heart's desire in shadows concealed,\nFound by the
brave, who never yield.

So follow the spark, let dreams take flight,
For in enchanted paths lies the purest light.
Where every turn gives rise to cheer,
And every shadow is a promise near.

Dreaming Lanterns of the Hidden Beings

In twilight's embrace, lanterns glow,
Soft flickers of warmth, casting shadows low.
Dancing gently on the breeze,
Whispers of magic among the trees.

The hidden beings, with laughter light,
Guide the wanderer through the night.
Glimmers bright in the cool, soft air,
They beckon forth with secrets to share.

Every lantern a tale to unfold,
Of wishes whispered, and fortunes told.
In their light, the world feels wide,
As dreams awaken, no place to hide.

Through silver leaves and murmuring streams,
Reality stirs in the realm of dreams.
Let the lanterns lead the heart so true,
To realms of wonder, where all is new.

So follow the glow, let worries cease,
In dreaming lanterns, find your peace.
For in thcir light, we are never alone,
With hidden beings, we find our home.

Flickering Souls of the Whispering Woods

In whispering woods where shadows meld,
Flickering souls their stories held.
With laughter lost in time's embrace,
They dance through ages, a timeless trace.

Among the trees, soft echoes play,
Songs of the past in twilight's sway.
Each rustle tells of journeys begun,
As light meets the moon and the day is done.

Through misty paths where dreams collide,
They weave through the night, a gentle tide.
Silhouettes merge in the heart's deep call,
Flickering souls, we rise and fall.

With every step on the soft, dark ground,
Hushed secrets linger without a sound.
A world alive with the breath of grace,
In whispering woods, we find our place.

So let your heart follow the glowing trails,
Through tales of wonder, where the spirit sails.
For flickering souls are the essence inside,
Awakening magic, where dreams abide.

Veiling Glow of the Mythic Night

In the mythic night where legends sigh,
Veiling glow of stars fills the sky.
A tapestry woven with dreams of old,
In silver threads, the tales are told.

Mysterious shadows dance and twine,
Amidst the quiet, ancient divine.
With every heartbeat, a story unfolds,
Of heroes, of monsters, of treasure untold.

Through enchanted glades where whispers call,
The veil of night cradles it all.
A soft, gentle hush paints the land,
With mysteries waiting, hand in hand.

So wander close where the nightbirds sing,
Embrace the magic that night can bring.
For in every shadow, a spark does lie,
Beneath the veiling glow of the endless sky.

So let your spirit roam, be bold and free,
In the mythic night, find your destiny.
For the stars are the guides, the moon your light,
In the veiling glow, seek your heart's flight.

Subtle Echoes of the Moonlit Hollow

In the hollow where whispers blend,
Gentle breezes weave and send,
Echoes softly twirl and glide,
Where dreams and shadows coincide.

Moonlight drapes the ancient trees,
Casting spells with every breeze,
Softly shining on the ground,
In this space, lost gems are found.

A flicker here, a rustle there,
Secret music fills the air,
As fables born from dusk arise,
Beneath the shroud of velvet skies.

Each footstep stirs the silent night,
Guided by the silver light,
Where time bends and stories flow,
In the heart of moonlit glow.

Crickets sing their lullabies,
While starlit secrets softly rise,
In this realm of dreams demure,
All is magic, all is pure.

Faery Glows in the Shade

In the downy folds of shade,
Faeries dance, a secret trade,
Glimmers spark in silver trails,
Where twilight's breath tells secret tales.

Petals sway with gentle grace,
In this ever-hushed embrace,
Murmurs of the woodland speak,
Of forgotten times we seek.

The dappled light, a playful tease,
Sways the hearts of ancient trees,
Gifts of joy, in shimmering heat,
Whisper softly at our feet.

They flit like dreams, not yet caught,
Through storied realms of whimsy wrought,
In the dusk, their laughter plays,
In the dim and loaded haze.

So take heed and look away,
To find the faery glows at play,
In shadows deep where secrets hide,
A world of wonder, side by side.

Shadows of Light in the Enchanted Glade

Amidst the dance of light and shade,
Lies a realm of dreams half-made,
Where shadows weave their mystic lace,
And time dilates in this warm space.

Overhead, the branches sway,
Feathered whispers seem to play,
Each moment glimmers with delight,
In the hush of fading light.

In the glade, the silence sings,
Of ancient lore and hidden things,
Bright petals flutter, lost in air,
While spirits hover everywhere.

Luminous shapes in soft repose,
Glide unseen where the river flows,
Guiding hearts to find the way,
In the magic of the day.

So listen close and tread with care,
As shadows dance and dreams ensnare,
For in this glade where all is bright,
Shadows hold the gift of light.

Shimmering Threads of Time's Tapestry

In the loom of days gone past,
Shimmering threads are woven fast,
Each moment stitched with threads aglow,
In patterns only dreamers know.

Cascades of light and colors blend,
A story woven without end,
Where laughter lingers like perfume,
And echoes burst with sweetened bloom.

Fleeting glimpses, whispers, sighs,
Forming symphonies in the skies,
Entwined destinies, a fragile lace,
In the weave of time and space.

Each thread a memory once worn,
A spark of joy, a heart reborn,
Fables spun from twilight's glow,
In the tapestry we all bestow.

So let us weave with hearts divine,
A fabric rich with love's design,
For in each thread, a tale shall gleam,
Shimmering bright as we dare to dream.

Flickering Wishes After Dusk

In twilight's embrace, whispers sigh,
Flickering wishes, like stars in the sky.
Moonlight bathes the world in grace,
While dreams take wing in the shadowed space.

The night unfolds its mystic veil,
Stories woven in the gentle gale.
Each glimmering hope, a flicker of fate,
Guiding the lost, before it's too late.

Through darkened woods where magic sleeps,
The heart of the night, a secret keeps.
With every flicker, a promise is made,
In the quiet twilight, where dreams are laid.

Stars spill laughter in a cosmic dance,
Inviting the world to dream and to prance.
Flickering wishes painted bright,
Illuminate the pathways of the night.

So gather your hopes, let them take flight,
In the soft embrace of silver light.
For in the dark, there's magic to find,
Flickering wishes, a tapestry twined.

Serene Glow of Forgotten Realms

In a realm where whispers softly play,
A serene glow guides the lost to stay.
Ancient trees with tales untold,
Shelter the dreams of the brave and bold.

Rippling waters shimmer with delight,
Reflecting the calm of the star-kissed night.
A silence echoes, profound and wide,
As secrets of ages in shadows abide.

Golden rays through canopies weave,
Painting the air with what hearts believe.
A tapestry spun from soft, subtle threads,
Where magic lingers and adventure spreads.

Lanterns of fate light the winding way,
Unraveling worlds where the lost dare to play.
Each path a promise, each corner a chance,
In the serene glow, wanderers dance.

Forgotten realms wait for stories to bloom,
In gardens of wonder, life's sweet perfume.
Awake, dreamers, to what can still be,
For in this realm, your spirit is free.

Secrets in the Ethereal Glow

In the hush of night, where the shadows sing,
Secrets glimmer, on silken wings.
Ethereal glow enchants the air,
Whispering tales of love and despair.

Glimmers of light flicker in the trees,
Carrying echoes on the midnight breeze.
The stars conspire in a luminous dance,
Inviting dreamers to take a chance.

With every step, a mystery unfolds,
In the heart of darkness, a light that holds.
Ethereal whispers call out your name,
Leading you closer to the heart of the game.

Beneath the moon's watchful, silver eye,
Secrets twirl, as the night drifts by.
Each sigh and shimmer, a soft-spoken truth,
In the ghostly glow of eternal youth.

So wander softly, in night's embrace,
Let the secrets of light reveal their grace.
For in the glow, where shadows collide,
Lies the magic of dreams, foreverides.

Illuminated Dreams of Sylvan Souls

In ancient woods where the wild things roam,
Illuminated dreams find a place called home.
Sylvan souls dance in the dappled light,
Spinning tales of magic that take flight.

Glistening leaves play a soft, sweet tune,
As twilight whispers secrets to the moon.
In the heart of the woods, where shadows blend,
Dreams come alive and old myths transcend.

Paths woven by starlight beckon the brave,
Guiding lost spirits to the solace they crave.
Illuminated visions, tender and bright,
Charm the heart in the depths of the night.

From blossoms of hope, new worlds are spun,
Every heartbeat echoes with what's yet to come.
Sylvan souls roam where dreams intertwine,
Beneath the canopy, fate's design.

So linger in twilight, where fantasies glide,
And let the embrace of magic be your guide.
For in these woods, both fragile and wise,
Illuminated dreams hold the brightest skies.

Murmurs of the Hidden Grove

In whispers soft the secrets flow,
The hidden grove where lost things go.
Where ancient trees with stories weave,
And woodland spirits dance and breathe.

A breeze that carries laughter light,
Among the ferns, in shadows bright.
Here dreams are spun with silver thread,
Awakened paths where few have tread.

The shimmer of a distant star,
Guides weary souls from near and far.
With every step, a gentle song,
Entwines the heart, where hearts belong.

A world of wonder, soft and green,
Where time is hushed, and fate unseen.
Each leaf a whisper, soft and sly,
In hidden grove neath twilight sky.

So linger not, but seek the way,
To find the magic of today.
For in the grove, with every breath,
Awaits the life, alive from death.

Dancing Lights in the Twilight Realm

Beneath the arch of twilight calm,
The fireflies weave their magic balm.
Their glow a dance, a flickering charm,
That stirs the heart and holds it warm.

In twilight's hush, the shadows blend,
Where memories linger, round the bend.
The stars awaken, one by one,
As day surrenders to the night spun.

Each glimmering light a wish untold,
A twinkle of dreams both brave and bold.
In this realm, where secrets twine,
The dance of fate begins to shine.

With every pulse, the night resounds,
In echoes soft, where joy abounds.
The laughter of the nightingale,
Flows through the air, a sweet exhale.

So gather round, and hold your breath,
For in this light, you'll find what's left.
A legacy of love and grace,
In twilight's arms, find your true place.

Subtle Radiance of Lost Lore

In pages worn, where stories fade,
A subtle glow of truths conveyed.
Each line a whisper from the past,
A flicker of hope held fast.

The tome of old, with secrets sprawl,
Holds wisdom deep, beyond the call.
With every turn, the magic grows,
In corners dark, where no one goes.

The ancients speak in twilight's breath,
Revealing life entwined with death.
In woven tales, the dreams ignite,
Illuminating shadows of night.

Each sentence glows, a beacon bright,
Guiding the lost to find the light.
For in these words, lore deeply sung,
Awakens hearts that once were young.

So lift the veil, and read with care,
The subtle radiance, truth laid bare.
In every page, a journey waits,
Through lost lore's dance, and woven fates.

Enchanted Shadows in Stillness

In stillness locked, where shadows play,
An enchanted realm begins to sway.
The whispered sighs of twilight night,
Hold secrets wrapped in fading light.

Where moonbeams touch the cool, soft ground,
And mystic songs of night abound.
In hush of breath, the night unfolds,
A tapestry of dreams retold.

Each silhouette, a story waits,
Of love and loss behind closed gates.
The stars align in cosmic dance,
Inviting hearts to take a chance.

In enchanted shadows, doubts set free,
To find the path of what could be.
For every dark, the light shall trace,
In stillness, find your truest grace.

So linger long in twilight's breath,
For magic thrives where shadows rest.
In every pulse of midnight air,
Awaits the dreams we long to share.

Enigmatic Light in the Fae Spectra

In the glade where shadows dance,
A flicker glows, it sways like chance.
Soft glimmers weave through trees entwined,
Secrets of the night combined.

Glistening hues of emerald green,
Whispers of wonders yet unseen.
Each spark a tale, each pulse a song,
Where the heart of magic throngs.

Beneath the boughs, where dreams take flight,
The fae unveil their sacred light.
With laughter low, and glances keen,
They greet the dusk, where hopes convene.

A symphony of softest sighs,
Echoes beneath the starry skies.
Each flicker casts a spell divine,
In the realm where starlit souls entwine.

As twilight fades, their essence grows,
A tapestry of life unfolds.
In every shimmer, joy takes form,
Caressed by fate, forever warm.

Woven Whispers of Twilight's Embrace

In twilight's fold, where shadows play,
The whispers weave, and dreams sway.
Softly spoken in hushed refrains,
Echoes of love, where heart remains.

Petals unfurl in the dimming light,
Inviting souls to dance through night.
A gentle breeze, tender and bold,
Carries the secrets that long behold.

Stars awaken in velvet skies,
Painting the dark with lullabies.
Each twinkle a promise, a silent vow,
Binding the night, a sacred brow.

Memories drift like firefly trails,
Carried on winds, where magic sails.
The night enfolds in its tender hold,
Whispers of warmth, in stories told.

Lost in the glow of midnight dreams,
Every heart speaks in silent beams.
Woven together in fate's embrace,
As twilight breathes its softening grace.

Ethereal Radiance of the Celestial Folk

Beneath the stars, where shadows blend,
The celestial folk their spirits send.
Draped in light, they weave the night,
Mysteries glow in pure delight.

Galaxies whirl in a saucer bright,
Songs of the universe in flight.
Voices like silver, soft and clear,
Draw the wanderers ever near.

From ebony skies, dreams take shape,
Enigmas penned in stardust drape.
Each twinkle a truth, a cosmic thread,
Binding the living, the lost, the dead.

With every heartbeat, magic wakes,
In the gold of dawn, a shimmer breaks.
Luminous trails from eyes that spark,
Leading the weary through the dark.

In realms uncharted, time stands still,
The ethereal light, a gentle thrill.
Beyond the veil of earthly sight,
The celestial folk dance through the night.

Breaths of Luminous Nightfall

In the hush that drapes the midnight dome,
Breaths of light call the weary home.
A gentle whisper, a flicker bright,
Guiding the lost with tender might.

Moonlit petals, soft as dreams,
Glowing gently in silvery beams.
A kiss of warmth in the cold night air,
Inviting the hearts that wander there.

Through woods enchanted, shadows weave,
Stories of those who dare believe.
Underneath the watchful stars,
They find their glimpse of who they are.

Fires glow in the depth of night,
Sparks of joy that chase the fright.
Each breath a promise, each sigh a prayer,
In luminous nightfall, hope lays bare.

As dawn approaches, soft and slow,
The breath of night begins to glow.
Held in the arms of nightfall's care,
Lies a world that's always there.

Midnight Gleams of Otherworldly Wonders

In twilight's cloak where shadows dance,
Soft whispers weave their secret glance.
With stars that twinkle, spirits rise,
Beneath the canvas of velvet skies.

The moonlight bathes the silent trees,
In dreamy light, a spectral breeze.
Each shimmering ray, a tale untold,
Of realms where magic subtly unfolds.

Amidst the glimmer, wishes bloom,
Ethereal wonders break the gloom.
A flicker here, a flicker there,
In every glade, enchantments stare.

With every sigh, the night draws near,
A symphony for those who hear.
Ancients beckon from afar,
Guided gently by a falling star.

So wander forth with heart aglow,
Where midnight gleams, and dreams bestow.
For in this hour, the veil grows thin,
And worlds beyond the light begin.

Luminous Hues of Ancient Lore

In yesteryears where legends loom,
Lurking deep in the whispers of gloom.
Chanting softly, old tales abide,
Within the heart, where secrets hide.

Golden beams of stories old,
In hues of crimson and shades of gold.
Each chapter penned with careful hand,
Crafted fine by fate's own strand.

The flickering flames of a dying fire,
Hold the echoes of deep desire.
With every spark, a voice recalls,
The mighty rise and the destined falls.

Through every shadow, through every shade,
Luminous hues of time displayed.
A dance of colors on parchment bright,
Illuminating paths in the quiet night.

So gather 'round, dear friends of lore,
Embrace the tales that time once bore.
For in each hue, a life can soar,
In luminous hues of ancient lore.

Dancing Embers in the Woodland Mist

In the heart of night where the whispers roam,
Dancing embers ignite their home.
Twinkling bright in the woodland deep,
Where shadows play and the wild things leap.

The mist unveils a moonlit glade,
Where ancient spirits are unafraid.
With every flicker, a story spins,
Of brave beginnings and where it begins.

Flame-kissed breezes stir the leaves,
In swirling waltzes the forest weaves.
Round the fire, the stories flow,
Of dancing embers, and hearts aglow.

With laughter soft as a summer's night,
The woodland's secrets bask in light.
A tapestry of dreams unfolds,
In dancing embers and tales retold.

So lose yourself in the misty hush,
Let your heart race in the gentle rush.
For in the forest, time stands still,
With dancing embers, and worlds to fill.

Veiled Illuminations of the Heart

In the quiet corners where shadows play,
Veiled illuminations lead the way.
Each heartbeat echoes a soft refrain,
Of love and loss, of joy and pain.

Behind closed eyes where dreams take flight,
Beliefs awaken in the still of night.
Whispers linger in every tear,
In veiled illuminations, hearts draw near.

With gentle grace, the past entwined,
Mysterious paths, the soul enshrined.
In twilight's glow, truths emerge bright,
Illuminating the depths of the night.

Every sigh, a promise to keep,
Tales of treasures buried deep.
In moments fleeting, hearts will chart,
The veiled illuminations of the heart.

So cherish the glow that love bestows,
In the darkest times, its light still glows.
For in the hush, where feelings impart,
Lie veiled illuminations of the heart.

Subtle Sparks of Enigma

In shadows deep, soft whispers play,
Each riddle woven, dusk turns to gray.
The heartbeats quicken, a spark ignites,
A subtle dance of unfathomed sights.

Across the night, where secrets weave,
In cobwebbed corners, truths take leave.
The minds are stirred by unspoken words,
While silence sings of hidden birds.

Mysteries swirl like clouds above,
A fleeting glance, a hint of love.
In twilight's grasp, the world transforms,
As magic gathers in quiet swarms.

The lanterns flicker, shadows sway,
Promises linger where dreams may play.
A tapestry stitched from hearts aflame,
With threads of hope that cannot tame.

In gazes locked, a spark will rise,
The enigma glows behind closed eyes.
To wander further, one must be bold,
For subtle sparks can never be sold.

Flickering Dreams Among the Leaves

Underneath the ancient trees,
Whispers float upon the breeze.
Flickering dreams take wing and fly,
As twilight sings a lullaby.

Through rustling boughs, soft shadows creep,
Encasing thoughts that dare to leap.
A tapestry of hope unfurls,
In hidden paths where magic swirls.

With starlit eyes and wishes new,
Each moment glimmers, bright and true.
Among the leaves, where secrets nest,
The heart finds solace, learns to rest.

The echoes of a time long past,
Dance with dreams, and shadows cast.
In whispered sighs, the world suspends,
As night enfolds, and daylight ends.

Remember, dear, to catch your dream,
For life is stitched with silver seam.
As twilight beckons, be not shy,
For flickering dreams wish to fly.

Glistening Echoes of the Eldritch Night

In moonlit realms of yore and lore,
The glistening echoes call for more.
Each haunting note, a siren's song,
In eldritch night where shadows throng.

The stars, like candles in the dark,
Illuminate the uncharted arc.
With every whisper, caution treads,
Through ancient paths where spirits spread.

In quickened breaths, the secrets swell,
Unraveling tales only time can tell.
Here in the hush, the past entwines,
With promises spun in silver lines.

In zephyr's pulse, the echoes thrall,
Each beckoning wisp, a siren's call.
To wander lost in dreams, to chase,
The glistening echoes in this place.

So let your heart take flight tonight,
And dance along with the ancient light.
For in the dark, behold the sight,
Of glistening echoes, pure delight.

Shimmering Veils of Faerie Whisper

In twilight's embrace, soft voices hum,
Shimmering veils of faerie come.
With laughter light as dewdrops play,
They dance where dreams and shadows sway.

Each twinkle shines, a spark divine,
In realms where starlit wonders shine.
Hidden paths of emerald glow,
Lead to secrets the heart must know.

Beneath the boughs, enchantments sigh,
As faerie whispers softly fly.
In every breath, a magic spun,
Where laughter lingers, and hopes are won.

From silver leaves, the stories weave,
In gentle rhythms, hearts believe.
Through shimmering veils, the night unveils,
The quiet strength of hidden trails.

So follow softly, heed the call,
In faerie's realm, there's magic for all.
As shadows blend, and spirits twine,
In shimmering veils, your heart will shine.

Breath of the Woodland Spirits

In the hush where shadows creep,
Whispers of the forest seep,
Gentle rustle, softest sigh,
Spirits dance where secrets lie.

Moonlit glades with silver sheen,
Echo tales of what has been,
Ancient oaks, their branches bend,
Nature's magic seems to blend.

Mossy stones and trickling streams,
Cradling all the woodland dreams,
Fellowship of leaf and stone,
Every heartbeat, every moan.

Wisps of mist in early light,
Gliding through the fading night,
Voices call, so soft, so clear,
In the sighing of the year.

So wander, child, where paths entwine,
With every step, let magic shine,
Bathe in light, the day departs,
Feel the breath of woodland hearts.

Twilight Murmurs of the Enchanted

As twilight spills its purple hue,
The world transforms, a dream anew,
Stars awaken, diamonds bright,
Murmurs weave the fabric night.

Faintly glows the faery ring,
Promises of wonder sing,
Dancing shadows, wild and free,
Evanescent mystery.

Elves and sprites in playful jest,
Frolics in their nightly quest,
Moonbeams glisten on the brook,
Whispers dwell in every nook.

Silken wings brush past the trees,
Carrying a fragrant breeze,
Ethereal laughter fills the air,
Spinning tales of love and care.

So linger here, in dusk's embrace,
Find the magic in this place,
With every sigh and every glance,
Join the twilight's timeless dance.

Dappled Light in Mystic Meadows

In meadows where the daisies bloom,
Dappled light dispels the gloom,
Petals glisten, colors bright,
Nature's canvas, pure delight.

Butterflies on whispered wings,
Poetry in every flutter sings,
Sunbeams kiss the grassy knoll,
Filling every heart and soul.

Streams that babble, laugh, and play,
Guide the lost along the way,
Summer's warmth, the gentle sigh,
Cloaked in hues of sapphire sky.

Chasing shadows, fleeting dream,
Hope and laughter in the stream,
Life unfolds in every space,
Mystic meadows, timeless grace.

So wander through this tranquil scene,
Breathe in all the lush, serene,
For in each moment, beauty stays,
In dappled light, the heart conveys.

Celestial Glimmers of Faery Hearts

In the twilight, soft and rare,
Celestial sparks fill the air,
Faery hearts with laughter gleam,
Woven in a starlit dream.

Every twinkle tells a tale,
Of distant lands and midnight gales,
Whispers carried on the breeze,
Secrets float among the trees.

Glimmers soft and slightly bright,
Guide the wanderer of night,
With every step, a laugh, a sigh,
Underneath the swirling sky.

Flickering lights, a beacon's call,
Leading souls who wish to sprawl,
Through the realms where stories breathe,
In the magic they bequeath.

So join the dance, let spirits soar,
Embrace the wonder that's in store,
For in this place, where dreams take flight,
Celestial glimmers fill the night.

Whispers of Luminescence

In twilight's glow, the fairies dance,
With gentle wings in a moonlit trance.
They weave their tales on silver threads,
Where dreams awaken and silence spreads.

A shimmer bright in the midnight air,
Secrets linger, an ethereal flare.
With laughter soft, they twinkle and play,
Beneath the stars that guide their way.

Each whisper carries a hint of light,
Illuminating the heart's delight.
In the hush where the shadows fall,
The night unfolds its magic call.

A tapestry spun from twilight's heart,
Where every stitch is a work of art.
In luminescent, ancient rhyme,
The echoes dance beyond all time.

Shadows Versed in Silence

In the forest deep, where shadows dwell,
Silent secrets weave a spell.
Trees tall and wise keep watchful eyes,
As the whispering winds tell quiet lies.

Each rustle stirs the lingering night,
And hidden paths emerge from sight.
Beneath the cloak of the ancient oak,
Eldritch tales from the shadows spoke.

With every heartbeat, the darkness sighs,
Crafting dreams that become the wise.
A world concealed, a story spun,
In the hush where the night is won.

The silent echoes call and weave,
In the heart of those who believe.
A knowing glance, a fleeting grace,
In shadows found, life finds its place.

Glimmers Beneath the Veil

Beneath the veil of the twilight hue,
Glimmers emerge like drops of dew.
With every flicker, the world awakes,
As the hidden light in the silence breaks.

In corners where the wildflowers bloom,
A symphony stirs, dispelling gloom.
The whispers hum in soft refrain,
Like echoes dancing through the rain.

Each glimmer holds a fleeting dream,
Captured in silver, a fleeting beam.
As moonbeams flow through the leaves above,
Life unfolds in a tapestry of love.

The gentle pulse of the night reveals,
The softest truth that the heart conceals.
In glimmers bright, we find our way,
Through shadows deep, to light of day.

Echoes of the Enchanted Glade

In an enchanted glade where dreams reside,
The whispers of magic ebb and glide.
With every breeze, a story breathes,
In the rustling leaves and the secret wreaths.

The brook's soft murmur sings of time,
Echoing tales in a lilting rhyme.
Where fairies twirl in a gleeful flight,
Illuminating the softest night.

In twilight's arms, the shadows play,
As starlit paths light the way.
Ancient echoes find their tune,
Beneath the watchful eye of the moon.

Each whispered promise and silent vow,
Is etched in the night, eternal now.
In the glade where dreams take form,
We lose ourselves in the magical swarm.

Dappled Shadows of Time's Keepers

In the forest where whispers reside,
Ancient trees stand tall in pride.
Their branches weave tales of old,
Guarding secrets yet untold.

Beneath the boughs, the shadows dance,
Echoing dreams, a fleeting glance.
Time flows softly, like a stream,
Merging reality with a dream.

Each leaf a page, a story spun,
Of battles lost and moments won.
In dappled light, the past takes flight,
Winding through dusk, and fading into night.

The air is thick with magic's breath,
In every sigh, whispers of death.
Yet life emerges, vibrant, bold,
In the embrace of legends told.

Oh, timekeepers of the ancient wood,
In your presence, the lost find good.
Keepers of the dusk and dawn,
In shadows deep, we are reborn.

Pulses of Light in the Mystic Grove

In a grove where spirits play,
Light entwines with shadows gray.
Every pulse, a heart's refrain,
Singing sweetly through the rain.

Moonlit beams on whispering leaves,
As twilight weaves what day believes.
Harmonies of light and shade,
In cosmic dances, fate is laid.

Crickets chirp a night-time tune,
While fireflies flash like stars at noon.
Each flicker tells a tale anew,
Of timeless realms we wish we knew.

In the mystic, breezy hush,
Echoes call, compelling rush.
Where nature's pulse holds ancient lore,
And dreams take flight forevermore.

Step lightly on this sacred ground,
Where magic whispers all around.
Embrace the light, let spirits roam,
In this grove—our cherished home.

Nurtured Glows of the Hidden Way

In twilight's grasp, paths softly glow,
Where secrets lie and splendors flow.
Each step leaves echoes on the trail,
The hidden way will never fail.

With every turn, a story waits,
In the heart of fate, new worlds create.
Soft murmurs tread on echoes sweet,
Guiding souls with a gentle beat.

The lanterns flicker, soft and bright,
Illuminating dreams of night.
In corners dark, hope finds a spark,
Under starlit skies, we leave our mark.

Through thickets dense, a path unwinds,
With each embrace, adventure finds.
Nurtured glows will light the way,
For wandering hearts who choose to stay.

Behind each leaf, a chance to see,
The magic woven, you and me.
In the hidden way, together we'll dance,
Forever caught in fate's entrancing glance.

Chronicles in Silvery Strands

In the loom of time, threads intertwine,
Spun from dreams and moments divine.
Each strand a life, a tale to tell,
In shimmering whispers, we weave our spell.

From stardust born, our stories rise,
Carried on breezes, in painted skies.
In silver strands, our hopes take flight,
Chasing the shadows, evading the night.

The tapestry grows with each gentle sigh,
Woven with love, where memories lie.
Every heartbeat a stitch, a song,
In chronicles vast, where we belong.

Under the watchful celestial glow,
We trace the paths that fate will sow.
In every thread, a journey passed,
Binding the present with shadows cast.

So gather 'round, as night unfolds,
And listen closely to tales that hold.
In silvery strands, our hearts entwined,
A legacy of love, forever enshrined.

Soft Shimmers of Faery Abode

In the glen where secrets weave,
Beneath the boughs that softly heave,
Whispers dance on the gentle breeze,
As twilight sighs through ancient trees.

Glimmers touch the dew-lit grass,
Where time and magic sweetly pass,
With faery laughter, light as air,
In twilight's glow, their hearts lay bare.

Among the ferns, where shadows play,
The stars begin their nightly sway,
To paint the world in hues divine,
Each shimmer, like a silver line.

In shimmering pools, reflections gleam,
As if to share a tender dream,
They twirl in circles, bright and bold,
Their stories of the night unfold.

So when the moon begins to rise,
And dreams alight upon the skies,
Remember where the faeries rest,
In soft abodes that nature blessed.

Ethereal Flickers in the Deep

Beneath the surface, shadows play,
Where mysteries in silence sway,
Ethereal flickers, blue and bright,
Guard tales of wonders born of night.

The water sings a soothing song,
Where whispered echoes drift along,
Each flicker, a story yet untold,
Of ancient realms and treasures bold.

As moonlight spills on rippling waves,
A harmony the deep sea craves,
With creatures old and spirits keen,
In twilight's grasp, the unseen gleam.

In swirling depths, illusions dance,
Weaving dreams in a mystic trance,
A tapestry of light and shade,
Where shadows meld, and fears do fade.

So listen close, dear wanderer,
To secrets held in waters stir,
For in their depths, the world shall keep,
The flickers of the ethereal deep.

Glistening Trails of the Ethereal Ones

Across the hills where twilight falls,
A path of glimmers softly calls,
With every step, a story twines,
Of ethereal ones in hidden signs.

They glide on whispers, veils of light,
Through emerald woods, in soft flight,
Glistening trails beneath the stars,
Leading us near, past moonlit bars.

In every sparkle, magic grows,
Where flowers bloom and soft wind blows,
Their laughter paints the midnight air,
Awakening dreams, inviting rare.

Follow the trails where shadows gleam,
For in their wake lies a shared dream,
Of ancient lore and secrets spun,
In glistening paths of the ethereal ones.

As dawn approaches, light unfolds,
These fleeting trails, their warmth enfolds,
For in their journey lies the key,
To find the magic, wild and free.

Dreamlike Luminance of the Glade

In a glade where the wildflowers sway,
Dreamlike lights begin to play,
A tapestry of colors bright,
Illuminating the soft night.

Butterflies dance on gentle beams,
Carrying whispers of hidden dreams,
With each flutter, a wish laid bare,
In the luminous glow of evening air.

The silver mist wraps around the trees,
Where magic stirs with the evening breeze,
In the heart of the glade, enchantment lies,
Beneath the watchful, starlit skies.

Each flicker weaves a story true,
Of nature's wonders, old and new,
And in this realm of dusk and glow,
The world becomes a tale to know.

So linger here as dreams take flight,
In the luminance of the night,
For in this glade of whispered grace,
You'll find the magic, you'll find your place.

Echoing Lullabies of Mystical Beings

In twilight's hush, the fae do weave,
Whispers soft, like dreams to retrieve.
Songs of starlight fill the air,
Magic glimmers, everywhere.

Moonlit shadows sway and dance,
In hidden glades, lost in chance.
Voices sing of ancient lore,
Of worlds unseen, forevermore.

Glimmering eyes in the dark night,
Guide the wanderers toward the light.
With gentle hands, they craft the fate,
In every heart, a spark awaits.

Through soft petals, secrets sigh,
While velvet breezes drift and fly.
Each note spins a tale profound,
As echoes in the silence abound.

Awake the dreams that lie within,
Let the magic softly spin.
For in the lullabies we hear,
Mystical beings hold us near.

The Soft Breath of Invisible Worlds

In whispers soft as summer's night,
Invisible worlds take their flight.
Beyond the veil, the wonders gleam,
Where shadows dance and starlights beam.

Gentle breezes stir the leaves,
Carrying hopes on which one believes.
With every sigh, a world awakes,
In hidden paths where silence breaks.

Dreams unfurl like morning's grace,
Painterly skies in quiet embrace.
Each heartbeat echoes in the still,
A harmony shaped by the will.

Glints of magic, soft and rare,
Invisible beings linger there.
Through realms where wishes intertwine,
The breath of worlds that brightly shine.

With every moment of pure delight,
Transcending time, they take flight.
In the softness of twilight's spark,
Invisible worlds leave their mark.

Luminous Secrets in the Dark

In the deep night, secrets bloom,
Luminous whispers dissolve the gloom.
Stars awaken with soft glow,
Revealing paths where shadows flow.

Glimmers of truth in the stillness play,
Guiding lost souls who've lost their way.
Every twinkle, a promise bright,
A beacon shining, pure delight.

Through veils of dark, the light does seep,
Where dreams and memories softly creep.
Echoes of wishes, lost and found,
In the silence, magic is unbound.

With every flicker, the heart takes flight,
Luminous secrets ignite the night.
From hidden depths, a story unfolds,
A tapestry woven with threads of gold.

In the heart of shadows, sparkles ignite,
As secrets begin to take flight.
In the cradle of stars, we shall see,
Luminous whispers set us free.

Hidden Sparks of Nature's Heart

In the woodland's breath, secrets lie,
Hidden sparks beneath the sky.
Where sunlight filters through the trees,
Nature hums in gentle breeze.

Every leaf tells tales of old,
Of whispered dreams and glimmers bold.
In age-old roots, the stories flow,
As petals dance in the sun's glow.

With each raindrop, laughter sings,
Nurturing life and all it brings.
In every heartbeat, nature weaves,
A tapestry of joys and leaves.

Sparkling streams with secrets deep,
Gentle whispers in the heat.
As mountains stand in steadfast grace,
Nature's heart holds every place.

Hidden sparks both small and grand,
A mystery we all understand.
In every rustle, in every sigh,
Nature's heart will never die.

Enigmatic Flickers of the Sylphs

In twilight's grasp, where secrets weave,
The sylphs take flight, as dreams conceive.
With shimmering wings and laughter light,
They dance in shadows, veiled from sight.

They echo whispers through the trees,
Like silver laughter in the breeze.
Elusive forms that spark the night,
With fleeting touches, pure delight.

Their eyes like stars, so bright and deep,
Guard ancient secrets we cannot keep.
In each flutter, a story spins,
Of magic lost and where it begins.

With every sigh, the air turns sweet,
In hidden glades, their shadows meet.
They beckon us to join their song,
Where we belong, where we are strong.

So linger not in mundane chains,
Embrace the light where wonder reigns.
For in the flickers of the sylphs,
Our hearts will find their hidden gifts.

Whispers of Enchanted Shadows

In the stillness of the night, they creep,
Whispers of shadows that gently seep.
Tales of wonder dance on the air,
In hushed tones carried with utmost care.

Through gnarled limbs and twisted roots,
Where only moonlight softly hoots,
The echoes of the past unfold,
In voices soft, in stories bold.

From crumbling stones, their legacies bloom,
Guiding the lost through the encroaching gloom.
Each flicker of light, a spark of fate,
Inviting souls to dance, to create.

With every breeze, a breath of lore,
Unraveled dreams from the ancient core.
In the whispers, we find our way,
Through enchanted shadows that hold sway.

So heed the call of subtle grace,
In twilight's arms, find your place.
For in the whispers, we shall see,
The magic lies within, set free.

Glimmers Beneath the Moonlit Canopy

Beneath the canopy, where shadows play,
Glimmers of hope gently sway.
A silver glow, the moon's embrace,
Guides all wanderers lost in space.

Leaves shimmer softly, a jeweled sea,
Where dreams awaken, wild and free.
The tapestry of night unfolds,
With whispered secrets yet untold.

In every rustle, stories dwell,
Of forgotten realms, a distant spell.
Dancing lights, like fireflies gleam,
Awakening the heart's pure dream.

With gentle grace, the night unveils,
Paths of wonder where magic trails.
Each glimmer beckons, a tender sign,
In moonlit dreams, our souls align.

So linger, dear, in night's embrace,
And let the stars their wisdom trace.
For beneath the canopy so bright,
We find our truth in glimmers of light.

Silken Glows of the Hidden Grove

In a hidden grove where silence sings,
Silken glows reveal the heart of things.
A tapestry of shadows intertwined,
Where magic whispers and fate is blind.

Dew-kissed petals, soft as breath,
Hold the secrets of life and death.
Luminous orbs that shimmer and sway,
Guide our souls along the way.

With every rustle, life awakes,
As ancient spirits shift and shake.
The grove pulsates with vibrant dreams,
In every shadow, a tale redeems.

As twilight deepens, colors blend,
The silken glow seems never to end.
In the embrace of twilight's shroud,
We find our essence, head held proud.

So venture forth, let longing lead,
Through hidden paths where hearts may heed.
For in the grove's soft, fragrant glow,
Magic awaits, and love will grow.

Shining Secrets of the Sylphic Realm

In whispers soft, the breezes dance,
With shimmering light in a dreamy trance.
Beneath the canopy of emerald leaves,
Mirthful secrets flow like gentle weaves.

Among the flowers, faeries play,
Their laughter brightens the sunlit day.
Each fluttering wing, a tale unfurled,
In the sylphic realm, where magic's swirled.

Through sylvan paths, shadows glide,
Carrying whispers of nature's pride.
In each dawn's blush, the harmony sings,
Within the heart of ethereal beings.

The streams reflect the starlit glow,
As moonbeams dance on the river's flow.
In every ripple, a secret glistens,
In the sylphic realm, the world listens.

So tread lightly on this hallowed ground,
For in the silence, mysteries abound.
With every step, let wonder ignite,
In shining secrets, hearts take flight.

Faint Luminance Beneath Celestial Arches

Beneath the arches, stars softly gleam,
A tapestry woven from a dream.
Faint luminance, a guiding thread,
Leads wandering souls where whispers tread.

In the cool night, shadows softly blend,
As tales of the ancients begin to mend.
Echoes of laughter cascade through the air,
Filling the void, like a whispered prayer.

Lanterns of hope flicker in sight,
Chasing away the glimmers of night.
Faintly they flutter like wishes unspoken,
Under the arches where dreams are woven.

Mingling with darkness, the light finds its place,
Crafting a haven, a warm, sweet embrace.
Each heartbeat echoes, a soft, glowing line,
Beneath the celestial, the worlds intertwine.

So linger awhile where the soft shadows play,
In the faint luminance, let worries drift away.
For dreams find refuge as twilight descends,
In celestial arches where magic transcends.

Twilight Sparks of the Veiled Ones

In twilight hours, where shadows weave,
The veiled ones sparkle, their secrets believe.
Flickering stars, like fireflies bloom,
Illuminate paths through the quiet gloom.

With every breath, a riddle unfolds,
In whispers hushed, the night gently molds.
A dance of twinkling, a graceful ballet,
Of spirits enshrined in the twilight's play.

Crickets sing softly, a melodious hum,
While echoes of magic in starlight come.
In the heart of the dusk, their laughter ignites,
Creating enchantments in velvety nights.

Through the veils of dreams, we wander with grace,
Embracing the secrets that time can't erase.
In union with shadows, we seek and explore,
Twilight sparks beckon, forevermore.

So close your eyes and let visions soar,
In twilight's embrace, find what you adore.
The veiled ones await, with stories untold,
In twilight's soft glow, let your heart unfold.

Shadows that Sing in Starlit Silence

In the hush of night, shadows softly sing,
Melodies crafted by the moonlit wing.
Their harmonies weave through the quiet space,
A tapestry born of starlit grace.

With each note, a story drifts past,
Carried on breezes, gentle and vast.
In corners unseen, their whispers arise,
Dancing with secrets beneath velvet skies.

Stars twinkle bright in the held breath of time,
As shadows embrace with rhythm and rhyme.
Each flicker of light, a spark of delight,
In the starlit silence, the world feels right.

And as the dawn beckons, their song lingers on,
In the heart's quiet echo, they'll never be gone.
For shadows that sing will forever reside,
In the starlit silence, our dreams coincide.

So listen closely when night drapes its veil,
For shadows that sing will tell their tale.
In every heartbeat, a spirit awakens,
In starlit silence, the world is unshaken.

Dim Lanterns of the Forest Spirits

In the heart of the woods, a whispering light,
Flutters and dances in cloak of the night.
Beneath ancient boughs, shadows entwine,
Guiding the lost, in a world so divine.

Flickers of amber, like dreams come to life,
Warding the wanderers from darkness and strife.
Each lantern a promise, a tale spun in time,
Spirits of dusk pen their secrets in rhyme.

With every soft glow, a path shall arise,
Leading us gently, with stars in our eyes.
Unseen yet familiar, the forest does hum,
A lullaby sacred, a call to come home.

Old trees are the guardians, their roots hold the past,
Embracing the moments that fade far too fast.
So dance with the fireflies, join in their song,
For under such lanterns, we truly belong.

Within the night stillness, let troubles release,
In the cradle of moonlight, we find our peace.
Dim lanterns will flicker, yet ever they glow,
Illuminating pathways where wise spirits flow.

Hushed Radiance of the Twilight Glade

In twilight's embrace, a soft shimmer unfolds,
The glade hushes secrets, in whispers retold.
Crickets play symphonies, stars join the tune,
Where dreams gently flutter, like petals in bloom.

The trees wear their shadows like cloaks of delight,
Guardian sentinels, under cover of night.
Moonlight spills silver on glistening dew,
In this tranquil refuge, the heartbeats feel true.

Fireflies blink softly, like echoes of sighs,
Chasing the shadows that blend with the skies.
A flicker, a brush of a soft, fleeting wing,
Hushed radiance dances, as twilight takes wing.

Adventure awaits in the depth of the glen,
Eternally woven, like mountains to men.
In the hush of the night, the glade speaks to you,
Of dreams ever woven, in starlight's debut.

As the hours drift softly, and twilight is drawn,
The world holds its breath, bidding night to stay on.
In the hush of the glade, where magic runs free,
The heart finds its refuge, forever to be.

Secrets in the Sylvan Glow

In the dappled light where the green shadows play,
Secrets lie hidden, in twilight's soft sway.
Whispers of ages, in rustling leaves found,
Echoes of laughter, in mirth all around.

Beneath the old branches, the stories are spun,
Of faeries and futures, and unbridled fun.
Every path leads you deeper where time
Lies cradled in whispers, like an ancient rhyme.

The moon casts a blanket of shimmering gold,
Each glimmer a tale waiting to be told.
Lovers and dreamers have walked these old trails,
With hearts full of wonder, like ships setting sails.

Foliage rustles with secrets to share,
Danced on the breeze, like a lover's soft care.
Sylvan glow brightens, as night claims the sky,
In this enchanted realm, where hopes come to fly.

So linger a moment, let stories unfold,
In the heart of the forest, where dreams dare to hold.
For hidden in shadows, beneath vibrant show,
Are the secrets of love in the sylvan glow.

Ethereal Breaths of the Faery Realm

In realms where the faeries serenely reside,
Soft laughter and music in flowing tides glide.
Ethereal breaths weave a tapestry bright,
Enchanting the wanderers lost in the night.

With whispers like silk, the air hums a tune,
By glimmering meadows, 'neath the gaze of the moon.
Petals of starlight in radiance bloom,
Embracing the shadows, dispelling the gloom.

Infinite wonders in every soft sigh,
Caressing the spirit, as time flutters by.
Golden threads of magic entwine and embrace,
In the heart of this realm, you'll find your true place.

Oh, take but a moment to dance with the night,
Let your spirit soar like a bird in its flight.
Each glimmer, each shimmer, a story unfolds,
In ethereal whispers of faery tales told.

So weave with the whispers, let dreams take their form,
Embody the magic, where imaginations swarm.
In the depths of the twilight, let your spirit soar,
In the faery realm's heart, you'll forever explore.

www.ingramcontent.com/pod-product-compliance
Ingram Content Group UK Ltd.
Pitfield, Milton Keynes, MK11 3LW, UK
UKHW021429220125
4239UKWH00039B/584

9 781805 645207